quick

*Books by Anne Simpson*

*Poetry*

Light Falls Through You (2000)

Loop (2003)

Quick (2007)

*Fiction*

Canterbury Beach (2001)

# quick

## anne simpson

McClelland & Stewart

**Library and Archives Canada Cataloguing in Publication**

Simpson, Anne, 1956–
Quick : poems / Anne Simpson.

ISBN 978-0-7710-8091-3

I. Title.

PS8587.I54533Q52 2007      C811'.6      C2006-905769-9

We acknowledge the financial support of the Government of Canada through the Book Publishing Industry Development Program and that of the Government of Ontario through the Ontario Media Development Corporation's Ontario Book Initiative. We further acknowledge the support of the Canada Council for the Arts and the Ontario Arts Council for our publishing program.

Typeset in Centaur by M&S, Toronto
Printed and bound in Canada

This book is printed on acid-free paper that is 100% recycled, ancient-forest friendly (100% post-consumer recycled).

McClelland & Stewart Ltd.
75 Sherbourne Street
Toronto, Ontario
M5A 2P9
www.mcclelland.com

I 2 3 4 5      II 10 09 08 07

*John R. Simpson*

# contents

quick

—are you all right are you hurt can you move how clearly men speak
through the blown-out window undo the seat belt undo the seat belt
and fall headfirst into the rain pulled from a wrecked car the side
of the road scarlet apples rolling here there each one a miniature
emergency a loop of cord a coat a scattering of glass hands shaking
water running down someone's face dark trees behind a van
brushwork on a Chinese screen a fire truck police car glaze of rain
this is where it happened an ambulance with its doors opening
into a throat of darkness—

Stops.

It stops—

Upside down,
he's moaning, blood in his hair.
                                                    Broken glass

grinds in my mouth.

                            Smashed air. The many clocks

of rain, slapping wipers jerk and lift of the tires the car silkily
veering off the wrong way on a wet road a long, vertiginous descent
frenzy of wipers this is how it comes gracefully the end of things
a guardrail a ditch a life closing with a little sound a *click* nothing
to fear brace hard the car slams into the rail on the driver's side
hooks metal flips hurtles down the highway on the roof the wheels
spinning like a chase of deer—

Stops.

It stops—

inside out bones showing against shadow white puzzle pieces
nestled one against the other delicate skull wide-open jaw sinuous
length of spine in the hospital a doctor traced

        smashed air. The many clocks

many voices are you all right are you hurt can you move how clearly
men speak through the blown-out window undo the seat belt undo
the seat belt and fall headfirst into the rain pulled from a wrecked
car the side of the road scarlet apples rolling here there each one
a miniature emergency a loop of cord a coat a scattering of glass
hands shaking water running down someone's face dark trees behind
a van brushwork on a Chinese screen a fire truck police car glaze
of rain this is where it happened an ambulance with its doors
opening backwards to show watery marks on the ultrasound yes
you're thinking it could be you it could be your bird heart beating
*now now now.*

Between

---

one breath, another.                                    *Transmutatio.*

## WATER, RUNNING

A hand, turning on the tap. The water runs and keeps running, blood through a body. No one stops it.

Water, running. A house fills up with water.

The police, the many angels of noise. The paramedics. They wade through the water, bringing help.

But the man in the blue silk bathrobe has already floated into the hall, past the grandfather clock that doesn't work.

All his life he's been learning how to float.

---

Like so.

I swam out of my name.

They put their hands on his chest. They bear down with force.

The man is divided: half of his body lies on the hall rug, half on the bathroom tiles. The paramedics do not attend to the way the man is sawn in half.

Outside, the driveway divides the lawn. Every tree in the ravine is a bell, clanging.

Inside, the man's eyes have darkened.

---

There's nothing to be afraid of. I went on ahead to make sure.

A woman speaks quietly to members of the family. She opens folding doors onto a pebbled beach by the ocean.

Not a king, lying in the boat with the curved prow.

Not a warrior.

Lay your hands on his head.

Speak the words. Push the boat to the edge of water; stand beside it. Let the boat be circled by night, above and below.

Listen.

A man is translating himself.

In full darkness, bring torches.

Lower them to the boat.

Set it adrift, flaming.

A wooden box with a key.
————————————— Inside, ashes. Box of frost. —————————————
O wooden box with a key.

I stepped out of the charred boat, walked into distance.

You must have walked over the ice to get here.

But you're wearing slippers, leather ones you've had for thirty years.
Only a silk robe to keep you warm.

And it's snowing.

Why do you open your arms, beckoning,
as if you were hosting a party?

Daughter.

# Unfathered

daughter.

Small as an eye tooth, smallest. Resist the gods. Be tissue-thin, purple hidden in green. Paper crown, five-pointed. Pretty fool of May. Shaft of warmth, bright litter on frilled tongue. Enter. A cupped place to sleep, coddled. Nodding human, come. Rest.

## WILLOW PATTERN

Last night a man said he'd wanted to live inside a patterned plate
when he was young. I remembered the blue willow, the stream with
its curving bridge and, not so far away, a pagoda. In the evening,
people lay by the stream thinking of how hard grass worked,
pushing itself up. The language of that country was complicated.
The seven declensions could only be learned by listening to water
for hours at a time. Yet when the moon showed itself, gorgeously
brocaded, no one spoke.

## BEYOND

The man in the armchair said everything we do has a shape.
Everything we do has a shape, and it outlives us. A decoration hung
above his head, made of glittering paper, cut and folded to resemble
a planet, or a star to guide kings trying to make their way through deep
snow. The man spoke gently of his friend dying in Newfoundland,
and the decoration wavered in the radiator's warm updraft.

MAYFLY

Let's say you had three wishes.

I never know what to wish for.
Okay,
I'd like to be a mayfly. Buried
for three years in sand, then a few hours
of gossamer life. Jewel-blue wings.
Maybe that.

I told you I never know what to wish for.

Two?

Why are you asking me all these questions?

Three?

I'd like you to come over here
and hold my face
as if it were a cup of rain that you're trying to carry
without spilling,
or a nest of warm goslings, or
the Tisza River, which I'm reading about,
shivering bright with a thousand
wings, the skim of mayflies. Yes, just like that,

comb your hands through
my hair. Come
into the bedroom, close the door.

EAGLES

The woman with the gleaming head.
You know her.


There—two eagles above the beach. One, then the other.

Wind tufts the racing water, feathers air. A wave slides away, leaving
pocked sand. Rocks, half-buried.

The tide covers them with white, unveils them with a flourish.


The last time I saw her, she looked younger
than she'd ever been.


The large eagle swoops down to the eaglet, teaching it to take
flight, take

to air. It's not tenderness coming towards us.


Whatever you were going to say—say it.

WRITTEN IN ICE

Sunday evening
9<sup>th</sup> March, 1921

How to begin—

Anselme, running from the barn, over the snow between bare black
apple trees, down to the harbour, where I couldn't see him until
we hauled him out, heavy, wet—he'd been trying to save the priest,
who'd come from Pomquet on horseback. (The steeple of Sainte-
Croix: I see it from the window. Thin, a bone.) Father Benoit didn't
know the currents, how fast they flow under weak ice. How, when
a horse steps forward, shies—

I'll knead the bread, put it in the oven.

A drowning man attached to a drowning horse: the priest's foot caught in the stirrup.

Anselme flung himself on the ice, reaching out. The priest grabbed hold, pulled him into a rushing heaven. Blue-black water, a cold god.

Sitting in the chilly parlour by his coffin, I look into his face.
The clock *ticks, ticks, ticks* on the mantle. His eyes. Open, an August
morning. Now, closed. When he laughed, dancing Joseph on his
knee, he split sky. North to south.

I walk behind the hearse to the church, the piebald horse with black
plumes nodding on the bridle. The coffin shifts in the buggy.
The two youngest girls hold my hands, weeping. I don't weep. Lot's
wife turned to salt; I've turned to ice.

When I sleep, if I sleep, I'm drawn into frigid water, clutched by a fierce

hand. Under the ice, a horse soundlessly thrashes, eyes rolling

as it hauls a man, and a rescuer who can't rescue anyone,

always descending into the dream of his own death,

my own foot caught, so I can't break free,

a sleeper who can't sleep, who wakes

herself by dreaming her life.

How to begin—

DUNN'S BEACH

Light, a needle, slides through bare-limbed
trees at the top of the bluff.

                  Wind gathers,
disperses.

Across the harbour,
trees are flecked with yellow, scarlet. In the evening, moon
will come in satin slippers, so quietly

no one will hear. I rest my head on moss.
It's warm, close to the earth. Below,
the beach is fringed with honey-coloured
grass. Near the shore there's still a ring of stones
my daughter arranged last August.

                  Within,

she'd always be protected.

I walk down the slope from the windblown
hill, stand in the circle:
teeth in a witch's mouth.

Tell me, I say to the wind,
tell me—

But the wind
fingers the leaves of the wild roses, brushes
the aspens, the black spruce.

Water keeps moving against sand
like breath.

One thing passes
through another. Sometime, sorrow
will have its small-leafed shine,
wine red.

MONK'S HEAD

Toy boats move together,
apart. Closer in, one glossy-headed seal
noses up and down.

It's low tide, and scattered
below the cliff are rocks, razor
clams, broken mussels. The air is a shelf

of blue. Anyone could step over the edge
without falling.

I stroke the points
of a star-shaped aster, lit
at its inmost place. I eat it, petal by petal,
taste the small, hot heart.

How do we carry a body
on fire? How do we lower it to the grass, tenderly?

                                        I walk to the barn,
where hay is loose across the boards. Darkness,
stranded in the corners. Nothing here,
but still we're afraid.

If we put out the blaze in one place,
it starts in another. It burns.

                        Let it.

Past the broken
barn doors, a rectangle of daylight. And further,
the ocean, with its smooth gestures. A distraction of gulls.

                                        One or two
fires along the bones of the wrist.

A nest, woven with white down,
moss, sticks. I find it
while walking along the bluff

where sky is an open hand
joined to the elbow
of horizon. The sea rises, falls.

                                    Each breath,

a bowl,
spilling into the next.

Under clusters of pearly
everlasting, florets turned powdery,
I find it.

How does love make itself so small?

Think back. Think of the times
it was a box of lead

                                         which could not be lifted.


But here it is in miniature. Now anyone can look
through the delicate bones.

In the nest, put leaves from the wild
roses, petals from asters,
dry grass.

34

This has nothing to do with finding,

keeping. It has to do with what a nest holds
and doesn't hold.

Carry each one you love. Carry the living heart,
lungs and liver, wild sweetness of the blood.

Carry the bones.

Carry the fire in the bones.

**Breath.**

---

Breath could be bell a belled breath unbelled could be upbreath downbreath unbreath.

## THE SINGING BOWL

"What keeps this light from pouring out as light?"
AGHA SHAHID ALI

On the windowsill of her hospital room, a singing bowl.

She recalls two high, arched windows in a farmhouse attic,
light slipping from side to side. The house was tilted;
it could have been a ship, going down. People needing to be rescued.

Perhaps she's been made to promise something because of what
she's seen.

During chemo, she studies lymph nodes in the ceiling tiles.

Once she saw a farmhouse lanced with light.
It was evening.

37

She carried it with her. Radiant house.


There's nothing in the bowl, not even desire.


The chaplain's hands make shapes in air, as if he's building a house
of cards. There, he's done it. The delicacy of the world,
one thing balanced on another.


She's a child in the house of her body. The doors
open and close,
open and close,
open and close,
daybreak to dusk.


Eyes, mouth,
lungs, heart.

Light poured through the windows from west to east.
Sky, speaking.


She has a brass bowl, a singing bowl, on the windowsill.


It catches the light and holds it, depending on the time of day.


Her body. A bowl, singing.

## BEFORE, AFTER

### EURYDICE, ORPHEUS

It's time. The lawn is shawled
with snow. Beyond,
the strong arm of the Acheron,
muscled under ice. Soon it will break through.
In this world it's not always dark,
as everyone thinks. Stars send charming,
indecipherable messages. No one
can figure them out. At dawn,
when it's especially cold, people shovel
whiteness to one side. The souls that pass
in the small hours

go over the bridges swiftly. She picks up
her bag. There's no time
to tell him how the water, black
under pale green, bends around a frozen
bank. She carries
nothing more important than shoes, an orange,
one or two letters.

Ever since he arrived, each day
lengthening gradually into dusk, he's had trouble
sleeping. He misses her
more when he's with her. At least he's discovered
he's comfortable on his back,

looking up. Scenes of brightly lit cities
flash across the ceiling,

                              disappear.

Now what he wants
is strong coffee, the kind he imagines
they offer on round silver platters
in Turkey.




This place won't remember her. She'd like
to leave her name
between a fold of hills, where sky
surrounds, thinly, almost
transparently, a song
before it's a song.


It wasn't just the way he looked
at her. The way she looked back.




She said she'd be ready. He's not impatient
yet, shuffling his boots
by the glassy willow. Icy branches tap
together. He's whistling snatches of an aria
people used to hear on the radio
during the war. They'd tilt
their heads, eyes almost shut,
and start humming.

EURYDICE AFTERWARDS

She's underwater. It's spacious, deep;
the marble stairs spiral around
as they descend. Years ago, a boy floated
down, dying. It wasn't in her power
to change things. He'd thrown
himself off the bridge, despair
in his pockets. The least she could do
was stroke the childish skin, carry
the body to shore. Now she recalls

air. What it was like to breathe,
a cloak of wings, hundreds, wrapped
around her. She drew that mantle
over a man's shoulders, put the crown
of her hand in his hair. This is the story
she tells herself. It could have been a daydream.
Sometimes his lyre can be heard faintly
in the spangled halls, or maybe it's the last
of the ice floes striking the bridge as it passes.

He lies on the grass. When did spring
come into it? One hippogriff of cloud
translates into another: expanding,
contracting. It's all unreal, the same
sky and river, the scent of living
things. The last of the ice floes passes
on the water, shears in two
pieces against the bridge. He studies
his hands, bitten fingernails. Every
time he turns, he feels the stamping hooves,

the great herd. A man can grow accustomed
to anything, a change of seasons, each snap
of the moon. Even when he's stretched
out on this slope he hears a steady
thrumming. It's a long way off,
but he lies still, pretending. Once
he put candles in each window
of her body: a thousand wavering
lights. Back then he knew about fire.

FAR-OFF WORLD

Ceaselessly gathering, descending: snow
whirls, falls slowly. Drawn into the body, a breath
ceaselessly gathering, descending: snow

feathers each parapet of sky all the way down.
Ceaselessly gathering, descending: snow
feathers each parapet of sky all the way down.

An eagle circles once in the powdery air. Floats—
feathers each parapet of sky all the way down.
An eagle circles once in the powdery air. Floats—

wings tipped. Listen, trees are bending.
An eagle circles once in the powdery air. Floats—
wings tipped. Listen, trees are bending,

smooth-skinned with ice. A tuning fork, far-off.
Wings tipped. Listen, trees are bending,
smooth-skinned with ice. A tuning fork, far-off.

Such winter palaces, with spiral staircases,
smooth-skinned with ice. A tuning fork, far-off.
Such winter palaces, with spiral staircases

on the palms of your hands. Snow assembles
such winter palaces, with spiral staircases
on the palms of your hands. Snow assembles,

whirls, falls slowly. Drawn into the body, a breath
ceaselessly gathering, descending: snow
whirls, falls slowly. Drawn into the body, a breath.

ORANGES

He bought half a dozen oranges
a week before he died, but didn't have the strength
to lift the bag to the counter.


We ate them when we arrived home
for his funeral.


Large, sweet oranges, peeled and sectioned,
on a white plate. Running with juice.

# HOURGLASS

An axe, the heavy blade swung—
cracks the sternum. Icy splinters
at the shore. In grey-blue distance,
where the Cumberland slides
into the Chignecto, a darkly smudged
headland floats in cool light. An eyelash,
or a piece of grit, slips through
the hourglass: tipped
moon, pale sun. Glaze of tears,
breath. One cloud ticking past.

WINTER

                        A feathery cold passes
between cedars.

Standing, I glance at the shape
I made lying down. Body that is no longer body
but the skin of a wish. How do we get up,

                                        walk out of ourselves?

The wind picks up a glittering
handful, a powdering
of bone. It lifts,
blows away through the spruce.




If we're cracked open,
it's only because something wants out. Light pools
past the bridge, eddies and slips
between wafers of ice

in the middle. Moon's lid stays open
through the deep silences.

Such thirst.

I see it,
once more, when I wake.

Sky, ablaze with orchestra
pinks, pale tints of yellow.
End of winter.

Ice still covers the harbour. And now,
five deer. Frightened by dogs, they glide
behind the alders. At the point,
one, two, three,
they cluster backstage. One drops its head, another
moves close to a doe,
ears pricked. They're quiet,

watching. A solitary fawn
leaps. Tucked into air, paused

                              between a clutch of birches.

Down come the hooves
perfectly. Blue-white ice is inscribed
with a pattern of flight. One last

wish.

# BEE AND WOMAN: AN ANATOMY

WINGS: *Apis mellifera* (Worker, 27 Days)

Beating two hundred times per second. Slur of buzz. Muscles,
an athlete's, body swinging side to side. Lantern above the grass.
Four wings, hooked together, aftwing, upwing—ridged and
braced—forewing, hindwing.

You want to believe I'm delicate.

Quick riff between lavender, lilies, oriental poppies. I'm on the
threshold, the one who's out there. I can't get closer. It's a way
to avoid sameness, staying. Living in air, air passed over and under,
folded and pleated: the long pull, in and out, of a silk scarf.
I'd call it sex, a world, glimmering as it goes through. You'd use
a different word for it. You'd call it home.

WINGS: *Uxor et mater* (Female Caucasian, 43 Years)

Home, the body. If I have wings, they're tucked behind my back.

What walks on four legs in the morning, two at noon, three at night?

—

Try again.

Who sees things from above? No, it's always bowls, spoons, cups:
the table neatly set for breakfast. The back door flung wide
to evening. Out there, nested bowls, spoons, cups. Larger than
any of us imagined.

Time's up. Answer correctly and still you've missed it.

WHAT I LEARNED OUTSIDE: *Apis mellifera* (Worker, 27 Days)

Like this. (What is knowing but a dance?) Round, round. The comb, a compass for my pointing. Let me tell you how the honeysuckle opened; how I climbed into its quivering. I would have stayed longer, drinking the flutter of each thing. Where? Go exactly in this line, diagonally. Keep the sun on your right (even if it's cloudy). I'll turn and show you again.

Like this. Honeysuckle—

WHAT I LEARNED OUTSIDE: *Uxor et mater* (Female Caucasian, 43 Years)

I think of thresholds, how I go out the back door, down the steps
past the honeysuckle—dainty, outstretched hands—across the lawn
and into the shed. Here's the doorstep of age, with its rakes
and shovels. Where was I? My mother couldn't find me; I'd crossed
the street. A nun cradled me in her arms at the doorstep of
St. Mary's of the Lake, pompom bobbing on a knitted yellow hat.
Not lost, held. Where was I? Held between setting out and arriving.

MOUTH: *Apis mellifera* (Worker, 27 Days)

Nectar mixed with saliva in my mouth, turning into honey. Most days I've foraged. What do I have to show for myself? All I know is how to tell secrets. Clover, heavy-headed, in a far corner of field. Monkshood, wild orchids in the woods. Everything gives itself up to hunger.

What I bring home is unpacked quickly, but they want stories. They want endings with flowers. It's true I've embellished things. Memoir, with its dappled light, halfway between fact and fiction. Peeling back time's skin to the first shuddering touch, petals opening like sprung doors, inviting my tongue. Musk-laden dream of tasting. Let me start over—

Hundreds of thousands of blooms, less than a teaspoon of honey. Magnum opus.

But I've seen the silvery pitchers of air, tilted to pour. Creek, fur-lined with moss. Water finding its way around stones. The sipping hours. Such food.

MOUTH: *Uxor et mater* (Female Caucasian, 43 Years)

Eat what's on the plate.

Over and over I've eaten the real, made it into a frieze of shadows,
leaping, shivering, dying. Listen to the throat's rattle.

My mouth close to your ear.

This isn't the right story. This isn't a story at all.

You want, and don't want, the one told by the bonfire,
as the bubbled, ashy marshmallow falls from the stick.
A ghost with an axe,
ghost with one shoe,
ghost
with a tapping cane. Turn and look behind you. Now—tell me,
what's out there that makes you so afraid?

WHAT I LEARNED ABOUT RAIN: *Apis mellifera* (Worker, 27 Days)

Air turned to thrum. To slant. It's wet under the droop of clover, but the world is bound. Up joined with down. *Nexus rerum.* Streaming loom of rain between tree trunks. The Greeks tied strips of cloth to their arms: mourning, prayer, celebration. To free something? Tether it? How easily rain forgets us as it softens, pulls back into cloud. How it forgets. A hundred scents ribbon my body, drawing me this way and that.

WHAT I LEARNED ABOUT RAIN: *Uxor et mater*
(Female Caucasian, 43 Years)

That it's touch. Out of the nothing of daylight comes one watery
shape, another. The architecture of what's heard. When it rains,
the blind listen to nearness, distance. Rain's Casa de Pilatos, rain's
Triana Bridge—its entire city. Stamping of flamenco on the broken
eavestrough. Skirts and drumming heels and, afterwards, blackness
and *dripdripdripdrip*. Andalusia unspooling down a driveway and into
a drain. I stand with my eyes closed. You here too? It's as close as sky
gets: fingertips trembling over our upturned faces.

EYES: *Apis mellifera* (Worker, 27 Days)

I don't know skin from stones. I have limits. Even with two
compound eyes and three ocelli—jet beads—I can't see red. I'd live
a life of purple if I could. Your face, when you bend down, is slope
of talus, the sound of rock falling. Pay attention

to quickenings. Wind

strikes the pond, a water droplet strikes, makes a diadem around
itself when it strikes the pond. Patter upon patter. The swift things.

But you. The titillation of small, smaller (legs, wings, thorax)
yanked apart, put under the Dutch flea glass, microscopes made of
silver, gold. Oh, erotica. Swammerdam's drawings, his seventeenth-
century bees. A compound eye plucked out, facets shown in clusters,
the whole thing split, like a walnut, in cross-section.

What do you know?

See less. See much less.

EYES: *Uxor et mater* (Female Caucasian, 43 Years)

Left Eye:

Baskets. The usual tasks.

Right Eye:

Each night-dark fir hollowed out so light can fill it up. It's moon, but it's not moon. Light, looking back. It goes into days still crumpled, it goes inside rock and travels further, walking on raven claws, with its green elbow of loneliness, its rib of sorrow. It opens the boxes of sky, again and again, taking out the long box for river, the clasped book for hands, the tall book for hemlock, the miniature book for bee: the one here, on the curled fairy rose petal. It's mother to son, mother to daughter, body opening to what comes next. It's time. It runs the length of the spine. It comes to the end of bone and goes past. Suspended—

WHAT I LEARNED ABOUT CROWDS: *Apis mellifera* (Worker, 27 Days)

Look how we swerve, embracing our queen, our one thought. We swarm. We do not digress. We hold the crystal goblets of water without spilling. This may be folly, but we are committed. Napoleon's army, moving into Russia, shrank and kept shrinking, after Borodino, after Moscow, after Smolensk. Here we are, keeping the polished tray of goblets aloft, so they make exquisite ringing sounds. We're on the cusp of a cold front. We'll become a mere dot, speck of history, the further we fly.

WHAT I LEARNED ABOUT CROWDS: *Uxor et mater*
(Female Caucasian, 43 Years)

We're surrounded by the living. At the hospice, the man dying
of esophageal cancer asks to see the ocean once more. The hospice
worker drives him two hundred and fifty miles so he can look
at the rolling, white-flecked hearses. Things don't come together.
It doesn't grieve him. He remembers the times he played Red Rover,
Red Rover. We call Charlie over. The light is always in the sky,
but often it's hidden. A reflected tint of rose on mackerel clouds.
For whom?

STINGER: *Apis mellifera* (Worker, 27 Days)

As for loneliness, it shimmers around each life.

I leave only this. Three dreams. The one about flying, the one about fire in a field. Can't you feel the radiance of the small red welt on your inner arm? Surely you recall the third dream: the one about yourself, inside yourself, dying.

Let out your. Disbreath. Fear, a fear, a fear of—rustles underfoot. You are here. Here, you: underearth, unlit, unwalking a dry path. Between the living, the dead, underdead disliving. At the tips of their fingers, undone fingers, flames. Dis. Non. Un. On either side, they hold up their hands, lit, as you pass between. Hands they hold up, pass you.

## ANATOMY LESSONS

### HAND

He was six feet tall, give or take. His body was wrapped in white,
like cheesecloth around Christmas cake, keeping the rum from
leaking away. Only his yellow hand had been unwrapped, and I took
it in mine, weighing its heaviness. His fingernails, which must have
grown after death, needed to be clipped. I didn't let go. I held on
as if we were about to take the floor.

The woman opened his rib cage as if it were a door and removed his heart. It should have glowed. It should have made us cry out. She turned the small mango around, tucked it back inside. I recalled the kingfisher that hit the window: curled feet, shock of blue feathers cresting its head, a black eye, shining. Had I killed it? That wasn't the point; the point was the stillness.

I was close enough to touch his ear, his heavily lidded eyes. His
brows might have been brushed with gold. If he'd been Greek, they'd
have given him a wreath of leaves. Women would have washed his
body with sea water, and afterwards, hired mourners would have
sung the *kommoi*. There was an exquisitely drawn map on the inside
of his skull, with long tendrils of river ending at the sea. He'd come
so far already. Later he would glide downriver in the proud raft
of his body.

THE VISIBLE HUMAN

Here you are, arms splayed like Jesus, on a deathbed in a glassed-in room with an IV and a plastic bag of poison,

about to be whistled into what's next: an elevator with an arrow pointing down. You, who freely gave

your body to the freak show of science. Your one great act consisted of robbing a man in Corsicana, Texas,

of a radio and microwave, after which you hit him on the head with a ten-dollar ashtray. It didn't kill him;

you had to stab him with a dull-bladed knife that bent on his chest. But that didn't work either, so you shot him.

Now the poison flows into the three-fold skin of your name — Christian, middle, surname — ending your life,

though your body goes on without you, like Snow White in her fairy-tale coffin. When they finish with you, we can look into every corner, from the top of your head to the soles of your feet, not to mention

an appendix gone missing, single testicle. You were executed, frozen, sawn in four, covered in blue gel,

before they sliced you into thousands of pieces (each one photographed in colour cryosections) to memorialize

you in cyberspace. Now anyone can take the animated trip inside your body, descending all the way through

your brain and bones, the rest of the baggage. A final impression of a footprint remains on the screen after

it's over. That curving line of toes: a refrain of self-invention, though self is elsewhere. You've been turned inside

out: look how they've kept you going. But what are you doing here, anyway? You're meant to be nothing

more than cloud, scudding across air, pulled apart by a northeast wind. You're meant to be gone.

Skin wraps itself around the city, hoping for a shape. It has nothing of its own, only the refusal to fit exactly. A puckering of water, early. That shrewdness between the trees. So your fingers. So mine. There's no seam, no place where it starts. Mussel shells, with their ridged steps, their mauve hierarchies. It's too much to look directly at the sun, with its smooth rhetorical devices. Look at the details. How one thing contains the next, cupping it gently. Take any galaxy.

Take t | one or
two sh | o meet
the w | ertips.
Those | aps, or
Seattl | . Even
the sm | . Such
traffic | harsh
it is. S | wrist.
This | that
wome | middle
kingd | jovial.
I don't | there's
a scen | ar the
drafts | darted

> Bones hold things up severely. A willow tree.
> February. Concentrate on the tawny spaces.
> Whether a monkey's paw is like, or unlike,
> the human foot. A goat's hoof. Sing that
> elegance. In the tree, drape the frost-thin
> bodies of your ancestors. Call the crows.
> Marry the bones you take down from the tree
> at the end of winter. Speak in a cloven language.
> Unmarried words. A whiteness. Sere, frugal.

between the trees this morning? The palaces of its tracks will be locked in ice. So much ice gliding over the world, leaving patterns between the eyebrows. What if the inner became outer? A cape lined with white silk. An embroidery of inconsequential fevers. Your amygdala, with its folding maps of world history. Back story, they'd call it. Soon, dusk will come to eat the crinkled foil. *Gate, Gate, Paragate.* One last—

## BEACH

Under her fingers there's marram grass, blade-thin, and a straggle
of beach pea. Further away: the skull of a deer or a dog, nestled
in sand. The piece of driftwood, where she's resting her head,
is nothing more than a bleached bone. There's no telling what makes
her cry. Look at all those women, wearing deep blue saris, leaning
this way and that, in the ocean. Thousands, row on row. Are they
moaning or praying? They're trying to tell her something.

## SHOVELS

Beside the cathedral men are digging hard. She pays attention
to the way wind lifts the branches of the Crimean pines. Sometimes
the men seem to memorize how their shovels glint in the sun, but
after a while they go back to digging. Soon they'll come to an end.
They'll have a good-sized hole, and then they'll stand back to look
into it. She's waiting for the black crow, the way it strikes sky,
making a flinty sound.

## SAGES

There are pinkish-white pagodas on the chestnut tree. In each pagoda is a sage, his arms folded in silk. She passes the tree, listening. At first she doesn't hear anything. Whispers, soft shufflings. What is it you're seeking? They're moving across the polished floors of the pagodas on slippered feet. You have the power to kill, says another. She pauses, but there's only wind, one veil of rain after another. Didn't you know this?

BETWEEN

The ball of dung was impaled on a twig: the dung beetle had to solve
the problem. First it pushed, then it went underneath. Finally it freed
the dung from the twig and kept going. Sisyphus worked as hard
as this—toiling, toiling. After a while he began to love the rock.
He loved the hill. He could feel himself between them.

## MORNINGS

She's getting used to it. Each morning when she wakes, she sees fire on the palms of her hands. The flames are small but distracting. Whatever she touches starts on fire: the chair, the table, even the mirror. Now she's teaching herself to pick up one thing at a time, carefully. She knows it's a gift from the gods, but sometimes she wishes they'd take it back. Soon, though, she'll be able to put it inside her ribs and take it out whenever she needs it.

A WOMAN, AN OWL, A BOY

A woman. Weir of bone holding a fish-glimmering
heart, feather-tufted ear, night heel, marked
with a star.

Lying on the harbour ice. A woman.

Comes gliding, mute, an owl. Shorn eyes
tuned to the world, ice dazzled.

Clutched water. Cold. Layers of pale
jade. Below, the living, the dying. In their throats,
dry leaves are rasping. Ear
to her own body, a woman folds back
one skin, another.

Hears a boy, hands tightening a necklace of rope. Hears him
kick away the chair.

Hears the world stopped at the rope.


Her eyes fill with tears.

The owl finds her,
flies into her mouth as she asks a question.

The rope
with a mother at one end,
child at the other.


Gone into the unstarred dark
of her mouth, the owl glides
until the woman sees

with topaz eyes. Until she moves noiselessly,
lifts into air.

Held.


She's held by air. Hears silence, its shape
and smell.
Flies to the top of the white pine. An owl listening
at the nape of light.


Hears the boy, each burned
minute, skin against rope, rope
against skin, neck unsnapped. Kicking, he
kicks back into childhood. Claws, with both hands,
back through
brother, sister, cousin—

long:::the knot:::the knotted breath:::furious lack:::

the seconds exploding for lack no mother no father no bell of air in
the lungs no feet no earth no walking no mother no father no bell of

She hears the last, the gone.

Stillness, that velvet, around a child's body.

Hanging, feet in socks, hole in the right heel.

Stillness. Boots below, side by side.

A woman finds herself lying on ice, as if fallen.
Lying on a frozen bed, wingless,
in the bone weir of body.

Hears daylight's
howling.

Opens her eyes, gets up,
holding the body of a boy, an owl feather
against her ribs.

Takes it with her.

## ODYSSEUS AND CIRCE

We had no wish to harbour there.

                    I killed a white-tailed deer
on the beach, gutted it. The thought
of that creature, with its silvery rack of antlers,

stays with me. In the evening, fire
kindled a gleam in the dead
buck's eye.

               Fire starts as a secret.

               It can't help itself; it reaches out.

                       I saw one of them standing

              apart,

              gazing into the bonfire's white
heat. I could see his face, the way
he followed bright scribbles

in the air. I felt something plucked
from sky, dark as a plum.
I was dreaming, or else
I was dreamt.

What do we dream when we can't sleep? We hum,
but our minds are shadow
clocks. Night can't be measured.

A branch scrapes, wind rattles the shutters.

He came to me.

Each morning she wants to know
something new. This is a game.

She touches the inside
of my forearm
with one finger, asks me to name my favourite

colour. I tell her the forms of faith are various.
                                        She feeds me honey
on a bone-handled spoon. We could do this all day,
back and forth.


            I taste the light
coming through the window.

His tongue is salty. It surprises me

                                 that he's mortal.


            As for me, I know each of the languages
of endlessness.


It started when I saw him on the beach,
the crackle of death


between us. I could call it




love, but it goes deeper. Inside her
is another woman. Another,
and another—

Where do we travel
but into each other? Now I put my hands
in her hair,
                draw her close.

I forget the quiet room
of Penelope's gaze,
mauve shadows beneath each thing,

                            going beyond.
The way she stood
when I left,
without caring whether water lapped her hips.

What I have to tell him is too hard.



She stands at the window,
a strand of hair falling by her ear. Soon
she'll tell me I have to go

                picking and gathering among the bones,

fish brittle in the scatterground
of darkness. My own ghost, waiting.

But I knew this before I came.

I'm thinking of the moon, how it nests
between grass blades. At night I open him
rib by rib, slip inside. Gauze-fine wings of a luna
moth, fur
of a snowshoe hare.

He loosens my hair, fans it
across the pillow. I kiss the hollow of his palms:

home
and exile. There are tears in my eyes. I turn
into a cup, a knife, a cloud,

but he holds on. The body is only

a riddle. There's more.

Inside each question,
another question. Her arms encircle
where I've come from, where
I'm going.
Each of us is a threshold
for the other to pass through. She goes into the spacious
rooms, making me larger.

How does the moon

become thin, thinner? He puts his finger on my lips
when he leaves.

Last touch
rings the whole black sky. Comes to the end—

starts over.

MONK'S HEAD POND

Ocean upon ocean, drummed
with last light, the last
of the boats tracing its slow, half-finished

circle,
a Japanese brush leaving a mark.

                              Trust this
ground, with its mane of grass,
curled after winter. Cliffs, hammered

to bone, sweep down to sand: the ancient
marriage of water, rock. Paired
ducks criss-cross a pale sky.

At the slope of spruce we double back.
Haven't we been walking for years?

                    Now one of us pauses,
sees the other near.

So near.


The heron's antique wings are hinged,
opening, closing,
as it rises up the length of the cliff. Grey
against sandstone red.

Below, stones knuckle together in the swash,
water slides in. Listen—
tumblers move in the locks. Things turn luminous, disappearing
in the backwash. It pulls
                              through us, going out.




It's as though we've never seen each other

until now. Rounded petals
of wild strawberry, pointed leaves tucked in grass,
earth underfoot.
                              One thing holds another.

We're alone on the headland,
wide open, as the tide rushes away,
rushes, and returns.

Five rocks, striped black with cormorants, remain.
The tide returns, but not as it was.

The long carpets of blue have been unrolled,
resplendently.
                              We stand at the edge
as evening draws close,

clasped by the first star. The track behind the headland
winds around a pond, stiff with gold
cattails. There's a banquet,

chatter, snatches of song. A loon raises its head,
ruby-eyed, dives—

                      water folds smoothly over it.

Come. Open the gifts,
open the dusky, twilight world.

## OCEAN, OCEAN

Water moves around the pulsing mass, lifts, falls. The sea opens,
keeps opening, a world just beyond this one. No need of bodies.
Bodies loosed from houses, hearts loosed from rib cages, liquid all
around, keeping us afloat. We might be all *glissando*, with gleaming
domes and long, drifting tentacles, scrolled together. One floats
past, another. Then a plastic bottle, half-full. A wave flips the largest
jellyfish, glazes the skin. Here's the work of memory: slippery
remnants lie bloated, distorted. They're discarded, worn-out purses,
turned inside out. The one that just washed up is merely gut
and ribbons, flailing. Hands that try to tell a story—

Chorus

*Music. Water's passage.*
*It was easy. You could bend anything then.*

*Remember?*

and wind up dreaming. Under a magician's scarf of water the fronds,
undulating, embrace and sting. At sunset, they're tossed here
and there, squandered, shiny. In a quartz socket: one dead, unseeing
eye. Tentacles strung taut over rocks: Medusa's hair. Waves lash
the shore, clap stone. They draw and suck, noisily scooping the curve
of sandstone, driving hard into the pockets. A crowd of pebbles is
harried, rushed along the seabed. A woman muses, looking down.
She's half-in, half-out of water. The tide drags. Sand clouds
an underworld, so her pale feet are lost.

Chorus

*The tides shaped rock by stroking it a thousand times. You knew how to do this.*
*Your hands dreamed the Ordovician, Devonian, Carboniferous.*
*Such oceans. Caressing.*

Angel, animal? Wings, folded on her back, a tail below. She could be that glassy bell, sluicing through a channel to its death. One clear thing with its arms outstretched, as if this will change what's coming. Let's watch something else: a passenger stumbling away from the wreck. Taste of salt. Life slipping past. Everything is pulled away: empires of sand, a few spiny creatures rolling, small green stones turning, turned. They glance one way, another.

Chorus

*You knew how to live in more than one world.*

In the further ocean: blue and blue and darker blue. Ululations
of creatures who've never breathed air. A world arranged in *terza rima*:
one formal circle, another. We begin as fragile things: how little
we change. We could be glass. A *ting* of forks as we move together,
apart. She hears what can barely be heard. The tide tugs her ankles.
She hears waves opening and closing. *Inferno, paradiso.* Can you hear
that? How distant it is. A realm of sound—hundreds of millions
of years—past silence. What can't be voiced is locked inside, but
there's singing.

Chorus

*There are worlds inside your head.*
*And seas, moving from one side to the other. Music, with its ceaseless*
*speech—*

*Insists. Insists.*

*You could have been a god.*

And rifting, rifting away, a few islands. Remnants of Avalonia. She stands waist-deep in water, watches how it happened. Whole peninsulas pulled apart, like bodies. Arm, wrist. Ankle. She lays each self on the sliding table, lets them drift to shore. No one will know who she was, or when. So what? The sea clicks together; there's a far-off sound of goblets breaking into bits. Here's her life, what she has made of it. Parabola, cissoid, strophoid. Whatever goes forward and back, making an elegant trajectory. In water, a few bodies bulge and soften. There are things that shine. Some float, some sink. Still, the pale ghosts advance. How ceremoniously they come, one after another, bearing messages.

Chorus

*You could have been anything you wanted. Not merely human.*

*Here's the part where it repeats itself.*

The sky softens with the end of light. Reaching for something solid
when there's nothing to hold. The woman slips deeper in the water,
swims, snatches up her hand. A jellyfish has stung her. She gazes
at its lurid pouch, fringed with cream: doll-sized weapons.
Mute and deaf and blind, the creature glides forward as if this
was what it wanted all along. Lifted on a wave, dropped on sand.
A spilled sack. It'll lose its sheen, begin to stink. Later, a boy
will poke it with a stick, just to see.

Chorus

*Did you think you could miss this part?*

*Everything is sharpened around you.*

The ocean wants what it can't have. It tries to swallow the heart,
and what's inside the heart. A constant rushing. No matter what
we press to our ears, it's half-heard. There—that phrase, repeated.
The woman swims across the silvery foil of water. What's brushing
against her skin? She wants a body so sheer it can hardly be seen,
wants it to dissolve into liquid. Water holds her: she stands
in the shallows, wades to shore. Behind her, the ocean is an open
cupboard. Lower down, a chill, and deeper still, the place where
humans cannot go. Things get lost in the dim recesses. What
matters is the surface, the beautiful doors.

Chorus

*Three hundred million years of wash and rush, wash and rush,*
*wash and rush.*

*Return to the beginning with each breath.*

She steps out, dripping, takes the towel she left on the rock. It's late, later than she thought. Over there, a shadowy rock. Another. When did it begin? She tries to recall, but can't. Only the lightest touch, wave froth against palm. A beckoning. Push and pull of the whole black ocean. She's sitting on the rocks, wrapped in a frayed towel. You know her, the way she leans back, sees a glowing planet closer than it's been for thousands of years. It's time. Those who've already started out are vanishing, tangled together. She strains to hear the murmurs. *Inferno. Purgatorio.* Water, rock, water, rock. *Paradiso.* Above, a hook of moon. An impossible note held, held, held. Piercing, clear.

Chorus

*Listen.*

NOTES

I am grateful to May Bouchard and her conversations with me about the Acadians who settled in Pomquet, Nova Scotia. "Written in Ice" has its basis in the accidental death of a priest, an incident upon which I elaborated.

"The Visible Human" owes a debt to the U.S. National Library of Medicine's Visible Human Project, which has recorded, in cyberspace, cross-sectional images of the thinly sliced cadaver of Joseph Jernigan, who was executed for murder in Texas in 1993.

I am indebted to Lauren Slater's article in *Harper's Magazine* in July 2001 ("Dr. Daedulus: A radical plastic surgeon wants to give you wings") in the writing of "Ocean, Ocean." Slater's article examines the life and work of a plastic surgeon at Dartmouth Medical Center, who asserted, at that time, that it would soon be possible to make wings for humans from rib bones and torso skin. He also claimed that cochlear implants would allow humans the echolocation abilities of bats.

For the same poem, I was interested in Giovanni Pico della Mirandola's view, in his influential Renaissance text, "Oration on the Dignity of Man," that Adam might have chosen any shape he pleased.

## ACKNOWLEDGEMENTS

Some of these poems were first published in the following journals: *Arts & Opinion, Canadian Literature, Dalhousie Medical Journal, Echolocation, The Antigonish Review, The Fiddlehead, The Malahat Review, The Times Literary Supplement,* and *Vallum.* Several poems also appeared in a chapbook, *Mayfly* (2004), designed by Heather Benning and published by JackPine Press.

.  .  .

I am grateful for a Canada Council grant that allowed me the time to write many of these poems. I also appreciated the opportunity to write "Bee and Woman: An Anatomy" at the Leighton Colony at the Banff Centre. And I am thankful for a residency at the Dalhousie University Medical Humanities Program during the autumn of 2004.

.  .  .

"Bee and Woman: An Anatomy" is dedicated to Sarah Tsiang.

"Winter" is dedicated to the memory of George Sanderson.

"Monk's Head Pond" is dedicated to Sheri Benning.

.  .  .

I am especially indebted to Sue Sinclair, who generously read and commented on the manuscript. Thanks also to Sheri Benning, Lynn Davies, and Alison Pick, and to Pam MacLean and Linda Clarke, who helped with the public reading of several of the longer poems. I am also grateful for the wise listening of Kate Waters.

\* ● \*

Don McKay—my thanks for hearing the music beyond the words.

\* ● \*

Warmest thanks to Ellen Seligman at M&S. Many thanks, as well, to Anita Chong and to Jennifer Lambert.

\* ● \*

Loving thanks to Janet Simpson, and to Jennifer and Sue. For the love and encouragement of Paul, David, and Sarah—as always, my deepest thanks for all you've given me.

# IF

If the tangled hayfields sloped into mist; if the leaves of the poplars
gathered the many ears of sky. If a crab spider scribbled in the wild
roses. If light buckled each silvery board narrowing to the beach
and if the many trays of ocean could be balanced—and if I could
speak with the easy glide of an eagle, holding time in its round
eye, I'd thank you for being here, exactly here, at the edge
of the rolling world.